Crochet Blankets, Afghans And Throws

Blankets, Afghans And Throws Patterns You'll Love

Copyright © 2023

All rights reserved.

DEDICATION

The author and publisher have provided this e-book to you for your personal use only. You may not make this e-book publicly available in any way. Copyright infringement is against the law. If you believe the copy of this e-book you are reading infringes on the author's copyright, please notify the publisher at: https://us.macmillan.com/piracy

Crochet Blankets, Afghans And Throws

Contents

Honey Peaks Throw 1
Melissa Throw.................................. 12
Abimal Blanket 20
Pebbles And Stars Beach Throw......................29
Falling Petals Afghan.........................36
5 Hour Blanket................................. 45
Little Lily Baby Blanket 52

Crochet Blankets, Afghans And Throws

Honey Peaks Throw

Crochet Blankets, Afghans And Throws

Skills required:

To create this beautiful Tunisian crochet throw, you will need to master (or already know) these stitches and techniques:

Chain, Tunisian crochet technique (alternating forward and backward passes), Tunisian simple stitch (tss), Tunisian purl stitch (tps), Tunisian honeycomb stitch (ths), Tunisian knit stitch (tks), end row changing colours, binding off in Tunisian crochet, blocking

Finished measurements:

The final Tunisian crochet throw measurements (blocked):

132 cm x 153 cm (approx. 52 x 60)"

Materials and tools:

To get the exact look as on the pictures of my Tunisian crochet throw, you will need:

Paintbox Yarns Simply Chunky (100% Acrylic | bulky | 100 g (3.5 oz) = 136 m (149 yds), Mustard Yellow (A) #323 10 skeins, Misty Gray (B) #303 8 skeins

Tunisian crochet hook size 7 mm with cable (at least 100 cm (40 in))

or size to obtain the gauge

Tapestry needle

Scissors

The yarn used for this project can be substituted by:

Red Heart Comfort Chunky

Yarn Bee Tender Touch

Gauge:

Blocked Gauge: 13 sts x 11 rows= 10 x 10 cm (4 x 4)" over stitch pattern

Stitch guide:

Tunisian crochet stitches are worked in forward and return pass from right to left, with the number of stitches (loops) increasing on the hook during forward pass and decreasing during the return pass.

Return pass (RP) is worked in the same way for all stitches used in this project as follows: 1 ch, *yrh, draw through 2 loops on hook, rep from * until 1 loop on hook.

Edge stitches:

Right edge stitch- This is the first stitch and is not usually worked into because there is one loop on the hook left after completing the return pass of the previous row. This one loop corresponds to the first stitch of the new row.

Left edge stitch- This stitch is referred to in the pattern as the End Stitch and is crocheted as follows: Rotate the end of the fabric towards yourself, insert the hook under both bars (left and right) of the last st, yrh and pul.

- **First row of Tunisian crochet:** Insert the hook in the back bump of second ch from hook, yrh and pul across. Standard return pass.

- **Tunisian simple stitch:** Insert the hook from right to left under front vertical bar of the next st, yrh and pul. Standard return pass.

- **Tunisian purl stitch:** Bring yarn to the front on the work and hook, insert the hook from right to left under the front vertical bar of the next st, yrh and pul. Standard return pass.

- **Tunisian honeycomb stitch**: This stitch is worked over an even number of stitches and 2 rows as follows:

1. Row 1: *Tss, tps; rep from * to last st, ES. Standard return pass.
2. Row 2: *Tps, tss; rep from * to last st, ES. Standard return pass.

Tunisian knit stitch: Insert the hook from front to back between the front and back vertical bar, yrh and pul. Standard return pass.

Bind off: Insert hook from right to left under front vertical bar of the next st, yrh, pul and pull through the loop that is on the hook. One loop remains on the hook.

End row changing colours in Tunisian crochet: The new colour is added when finishing the return pass of the previous row and 2 loops are remaining on the hook. Yrh with the new colour and draw through 2 loops.

Crochet Blankets, Afghans And Throws

Stitch chart:

Honey Peaks Throw stitch chart and legend

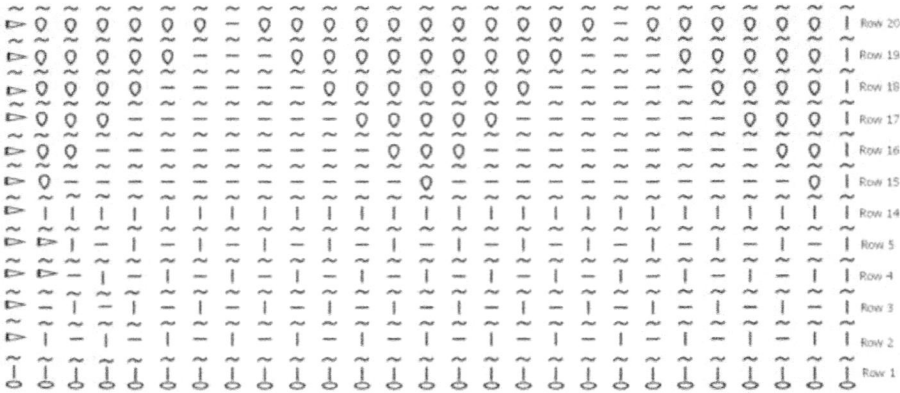

Crochet Blankets, Afghans And Throws

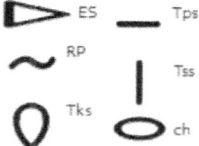

Notes:

Number of loops on hook equals number of sts for row counting.

The throw is worked flat with RS always facing; the pattern consists of two alternating sections: 12 rows of honeycomb section worked in Mustard Yellow and 12 rows of peaks section worked in Misty Grey. The two sections are separated by 1 row of Tunisian simple stitch worked in the colour of the consecutive stitch section.

Crochet Blankets, Afghans And Throws

Instructions:

Tunisian Crochet Throw

With A, ch 171.

Row 1 FP: Insert hook in back bump of 2nd ch from hook, yrh, pull

up lp in each across. 171 loops on hook.

Row 1 RP and all RPs except where changing colours: Standard RP.

Row 2: *Tss, tps; rep from * to last 2 sts, tss in next st, ES.

Row 3: *Tps, tss; rep from * to last 2 sts, tps in next st, ES.

Rows 4-11: Repeat rows 2 and 3.

Row 12: Repeat Row 2.

Row 13 FP: Repeat Row 3.

Row 13 RP: Ch 1, *yrh, draw through 2 lps on hook, rep from * until 2 lps rem on hook, yrh with B and pull up lp.

Row 14: Tss across to last st, ES.

Row 15: Tks, *tps in next 11 sts, tks in next st; rep from * to last st, ES.

Row 16: Tks in next 2 sts, tps in next 9 sts, *tks in next 3 sts, tps in next 9 sts rep from * to last 3 sts, tks in next 2 sts, ES.

Row 17: Tks in next 3 sts, tps in next 7 sts, * tks in next 5 sts, tps in next 7 sts; rep from * to last 4 sts, tks in next 3 sts, ES.

Row 18: Tks in next 4 sts, tps in next 5 sts, * tks in next 7 sts, tps in next 5 sts; rep from * to last 5 sts, tks in next 4 sts, ES.

Row 19: Tks in next 5 sts, tps in next 3 sts, *tks in next 9 sts, tps in next 3 sts; rep from * to last 6 sts, tks in next 5 sts, ES.

Row 20: Tks in next 6 sts, tps in next st, *tks in next 11 sts, tps in next st; rep from * to last 7 sts, tks in next 6 sts, ES.

Rows 21-25: Repeat rows 15-19.

Row 26 FP: Repeat Row 20.

Row 26 RP: Ch 1, *yrh, draw through 2 lps on hook, rep from * until 2 lps rem on hook, yrh with A and pull up lp.

Row 27: Repeat Row 14.

Rows 28- 52: Repeat rows 2-26.

Rows 53-156: Repeat rows 27-52 four more times.

Row 157-168: Repeat rows 27-38.

Row 169: Repeat Row 3.

Row 170: Bind off.

Crochet Blankets, Afghans And Throws

Finishing

Weave in ends and block to final measurements.

Enjoy your Tunisian crochet blanket!

Melissa Throw

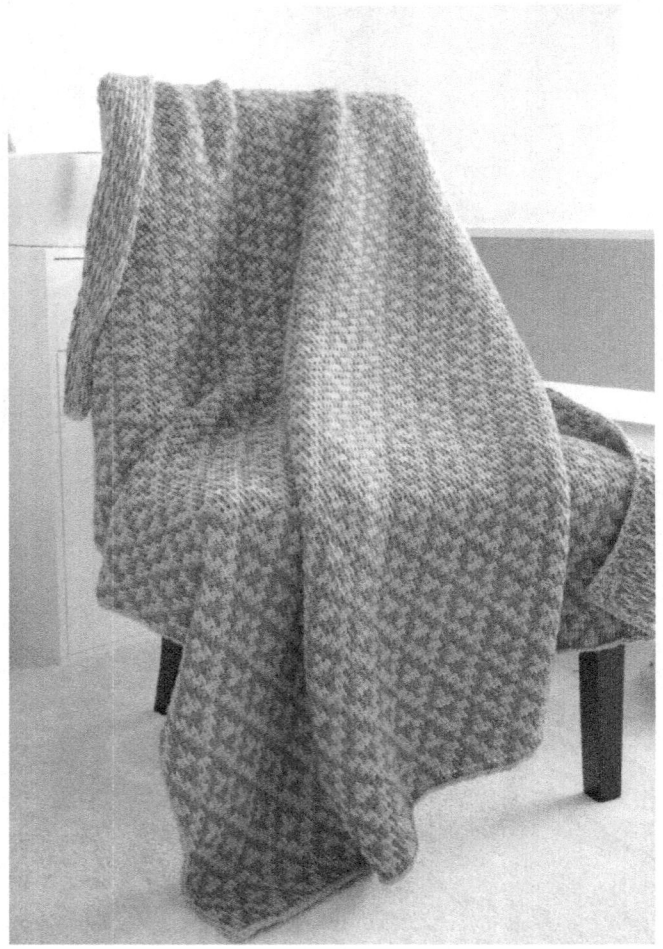

Skills required:

Crochet Blankets, Afghans And Throws

To create this beautiful Tunisian crochet throw you will need to master (or already know) these stitches and techniques:

Chain, Tunisian crochet technique (alternating forward and return passes), Tunisian simple stitch (tss), Tunisian crochet colourwork, Tunisian simple stitch bind-off, blocking.

Finished measurements:

The final Tunisian crochet throw measurements (blocked):

105.5 cm x 140 cm (approx. 41.5" x 55")

Materials and tools

To get the exact look as on the pictures of my Tunisian crochet throw, you will need:

We Crochet Brava (100% Acrylic | Worsted weight | 100 g (3.5 oz) = 199 m (218 yds)), (#) Almond 5 skeins (**A**), (#) Gingerbread 5 skeins (**B**)

Tunisian crochet hook size 7.0 mm with cable (at least 79 cm (31")) or size to obtain the gauge

Tapestry needle

Scissors

Gauge:

Blocked Gauge:

14 sts x 9 rows = 10 x 10 cm (4 x 4") over tss

Gauge helps you to understand how the project turns out in terms of the final size. If you would like to achieve the exact size of the final project as in the instructions above, you gauge needs to match exactly to the above.

If you get more stitches and/or rows than stated above using the exact hook size as per instructions, your final project will turn out smaller. Conversely, if you get less stitches and/or rows than stated above using the exact hooks size as per instructions, your final project will turn out bigger.

To make adjustments, if you get more stitches and/or rows, you can try using bigger hook size to get closer to the desired size. Conversely, if you get less stitches and/or rows, you can try using smaller hook size to get closer to the desired size.

It may take trial and error to try out a few hook sizes to achieve the exact size.

Alternatively, if you really don't want to make several samples to achieve the desired size, you can try to alter your tension as you work the project. However, I would advise to try this out once you master the basics of Tunisian crochet as it may be a bit tiresome to try to master the basics of Tunisian crochet and focus on alternating your tension while working the project.

Stitch guide:

Tunisian crochet stitches are worked in 2 steps; forward and return pass from right to left, with the number of sts (lps) increasing on the hook during the forward pass and decreasing during the return pass.

Standard Return pass is worked in the same way for all stitches (rows of sts) used in this project as follows : 1 ch, * yrh, draw through 2 lps on hook, rep from * until 1 lp on hook.

Edge stitches:

Right edge stitch- This is the first lp on hook and counts as first st unless otherwise stated.

Left edge stitch- This st is referred to in the pattern as the End Stitch (ES) and is crocheted as follows: Rotate the end of the fabric towards yourself, insert the hook under both bars (left and right) of the last st, yrh and pul.

- **First row of Tunisian crochet:** Insert the hook in the back bump of second ch from hook, yrh and pul across.
- **Tunisian simple stitch**: Insert the hook from right to left under front vertical bar of the next st, yrh and pul.

Changing colours as you go: When changing the colours within a row in Tunisian crochet, place the new strand of yarn over the old strand. This locks the old colour in place and prevent gaps occurring between the different colour sections.

Tunisian Simple stitch bind-off: Insert hook from right to left under front vertical bar of the next st, yrh, pul and pull through the lp that is on the hook. One lp remains on the hook.

Stitch chart:

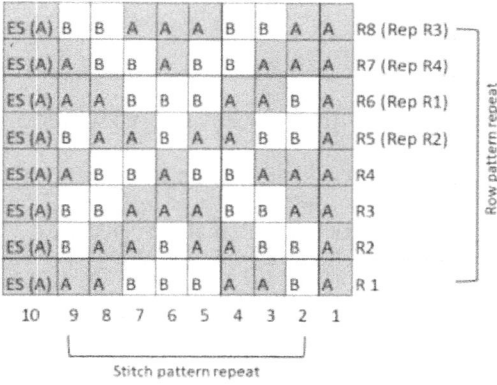

Stitch pattern repeat

Notes:

- Similar worsted weight yarns may be substituted; please check gauge.

- Number of loops on hook equals number of sts for row counting after Return Pass.

- The blanket is worked flat with RS always facing from bottom up and left to right in columns of squares.

Instructions

Tunisian crochet throw

With **A**, ch 146.

Row 1 FP: Insert the hook in the back bump of second ch from hook, yrh and pul, * insert the hook in the back bump of the next ch, yrh and pul following colourwork chart (R 1); rep from * across. 146 lps on hook.

Row 1 RP and all other RPs: Standard RP.

Rows 2-8: Continue working colourwork chart, tss in each st across to last st, ES in last st.

Row 9: Tss in each st across following colourwork chart (R1) to last st, ES in last st.

Rows 10-16: Rep Rows 2-8.

Rows 17-120: Rep Rows 9-16.

Row 121: In A, Tss bind-off.

Fasten-off.

Finishing:

Weave in all ends and block to final measurements.

Abimal Blanket

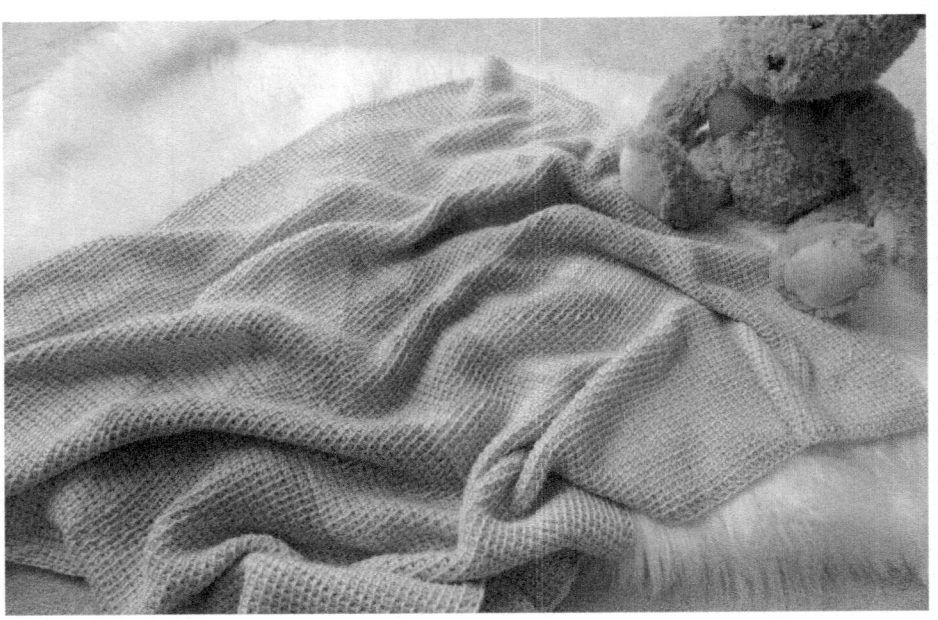

Skills required:

To create this beautiful Tunisian crochet baby blanket, you will need to master (or already know) these stitches and techniques:

Chain, Tunisian crochet technique (alternating forward and backward passes), Tunisian simple stitch (tss), Tunisian reverse stitch (trs), intarsia, stranded colourwork, Tunisian reverse stitch bind off, blocking.

Finished measurements:

The final Tunisian crochet baby blanket measurements (blocked):

70.5 x 80 cm (27.75 x 31.5")

Materials and tools:

To get the exact look as on the pictures of my Tunisian crochet baby blanket, you will need:

King Cole Bamboo Cotton (50% Bamboo Viscose, 50% Cotton | DK weight | 100 g (3.5 oz) = 230 m (252 yds)), #543 Oyster (A) 2 skeins, #618 Dusty Pink (B) 1 skein, #609 Glacier (C) 1 skein

Tunisian crochet hook size 5.5 mm (US size I/9) with cable (at least 51 cm (approx. 20")) or size to obtain the gauge

Tapestry needle

Scissors

Gauge:

Blocked Gauge:

Crochet Blankets, Afghans And Throws

17 sts x 14 rows = 10 x 10 cm (4 x 4") over tss

Gauge helps you to understand how the project turns out in terms of the final size. If you would like to achieve the exact size of the final project as in the instructions above, you gauge needs to match exactly to the above.

If you get more stitches and/or rows than stated above using the exact hook size as per instructions, your final project will turn out smaller. Conversely, if you get less stitches and/or rows than stated above using the exact hooks size as per instructions, your final project will turn out bigger.

To make adjustments, if you get more stitches and/or rows, you can try using bigger hook size to get closer to the desired size. Conversely, if you get less stitches and/or rows, you can try using smaller hook size to get closer to the desired size.

It may take trial and error to try out a few hook sizes to achieve the exact size.

Alternatively, if you really don't want to make several samples to achieve the desired size, you can try to alter your tension as you work the project. However, I would advise to try this out once you master the basics of Tunisian crochet as it may be a bit tiresome to try to master the basics of Tunisian crochet and focus on alternating your tension while working the project.

Stitch Guide:

Crochet Blankets, Afghans And Throws

Tunisian crochet stitches are worked in 2 steps; forward and return pass from right to left, with the number of sts (lps) increasing on the hook during the forward pass and decreasing during the return pass.

Standard return pass is worked as follows: ch 1, *yrh, draw through 2 lps on hook, rep from * until 1 lp on hook.

Edge stitches:

Right edge stitch- This is the first lp on hook and counts as first st unless otherwise stated.

Left edge stitch- This st is referred to in the pattern as the End Stitch (ES) and is crocheted as follows: Rotate the end of the fabric towards yourself, insert the hook under both bars (left and right) of the last st, yrh and pul.

- **First row of Tunisian crochet:** Insert the hook in the back bump of second ch from hook, yrh and pul across.

- **Tunisian simple stitch**: Insert the hook from right to left under front vertical bar of the next st, yrh and pul.

- **Tunisian reverse stitch**: Insert the hook from right to left under back vertical bar of the next st, yrh and pul.

Tunisian reverse stitch bind-off: Insert hook from right to left under back vertical bar of the next st, yrh, pul and pull through the loop that is on the hook. One loop remains on the hook.

Changing colours as you go: When changing the colours within a row in Tunisian crochet, place the new strand of yarn over the old strand. This locks the old colour in place and prevent gaps occurring between the different colour sections.

Abbreviations:

Ch- chain

st(s)- stitch(es)

ES- end stitch

tss- Tunisian simple stitch

trs- Tunisian reverse stitch

lp(s)- loop(s)

pul- pull up a loop

Crochet Blankets, Afghans And Throws

RS- right side

WS- wrong side

FP- forward pass

RP- return pass

approx.- approximately

rep- repeat

yrh- yarn round the hook

Notes:

The Abimal Blanket is worked flat, RS facing from right to left, with colours creating overlaying triangular pattern in the centre of the blanket.

To adjust the size of this Tunisian crochet baby blanket:

Each triangle is approximately 6" long (23 rows), so to extend the blanket, add multiples of 23 rows that will add an extra 6" (per each multiple) to the length of the project.

If you prefer to maintain the colour sequence of equal number of triangles in B and C, add multiples of 23 x 2 that will add an extra 12" (per each multiple) to the length of the blanket. To adjust width, add any number of stitches on each side of the triangular pattern (as per gauge, 17 sts is 4", so for example to add 4" on each side, 34 sts would need to be added to the basic st count, 17 on each side of the triangular pattern).

Please note that sizing up the blanket will have an impact on the yardage for this project and will require more yarn than is stated in the Materials and Tools section.

Instructions:

Tunisian crochet baby blanket

With A, chain 121.

Row 1 FP: Working in the back bump of ch st, insert hook in 2nd ch from hook yrh and pul across. 121 lps.

Row 1 RP and all RP in inc rows: Standard RP.

Row 2: Trs across to last st, ES.

Row 3: Rep Row 2.

Row 4: Trs in next st, tss to last 2 sts, trs in next st, ES.

Rows 5-7: Rep Row 4.

Row 8: Trs in next st, tss in next 58 sts, following the Triangles Diagram, start working the diagram using B, tss in next 58 sts, trs in next st, ES.

Rows 9-52: Continue working the Triangles Diagram (changing colours from B to C as indicated) as commenced in Row 8 working 1 trs at the beginning and 1 trs before the ES in each Row.

Rows 53-82: Rep Rows 23-52.

Rows 83-105: Rep Rows 23-45.

Row 106-110: Rep Row 4.

Rows 111-112: Rep Row 2.

Row 113: Tunisian reverse stitch bind-off.

Finishing:

Weave in ends and block to final measurements.

Diagram:

Crochet Blankets, Afghans And Throws

Triangles Diagram

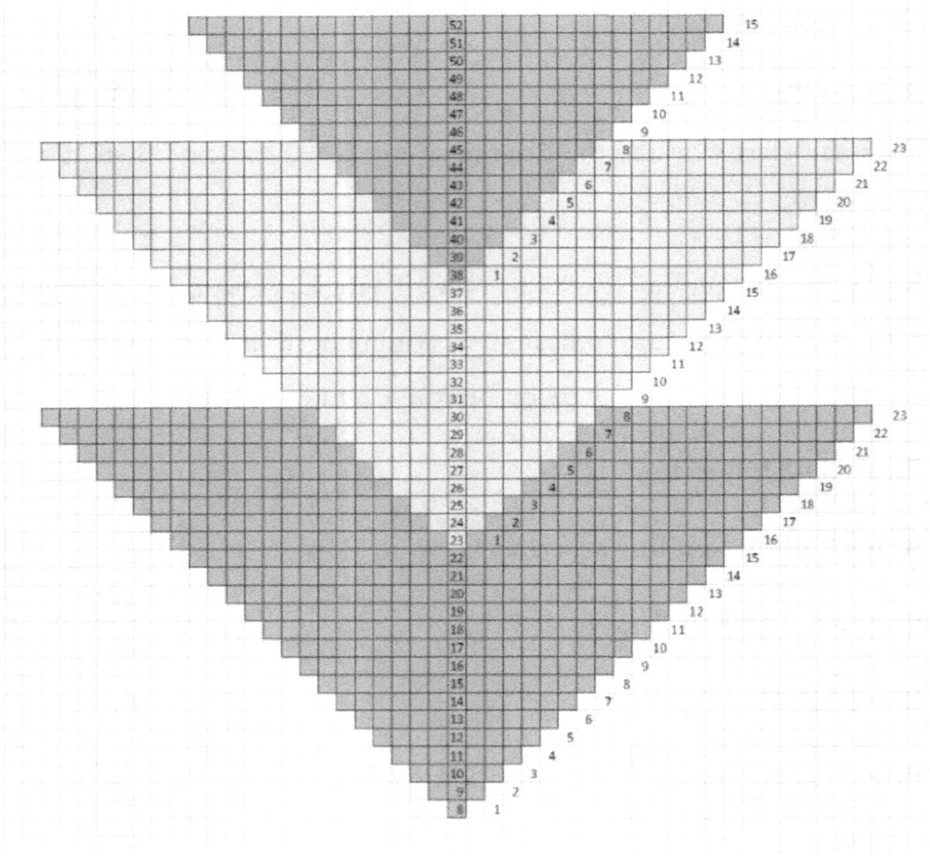

B
C

Pebbles And Stars Beach Throw

Skills required

Chain, Single crochet (sc), Foundation single crochet (fsc), First linked treble crochet (fltc), Linked treble crochet (ltc), Bobble stitch (bo), First star stitch (fstr), Star stitch (str), blocking.

Finished measurements

The final blanket measurements (blocked):

Crochet Blankets, Afghans And Throws

112 x 140 cm (approx. 44 x 55 in)

Materials and tools

Caron Simply Soft (100% Acrylic | Worsted weight | 170.1 g (6 oz) = 288 m (315 yds)), Ocean (#9759) A 4 skeins, Bone (#9703) B 3 skeins, Persimmon (#9754) C 3 skeins

Crochet hook size 5.0 mm (US size H-8) size to obtain the gauge

Tapestry needle

Scissors

Gauge

Blocked Gauge:

14 sts and 9.5 rows = 10 x 10 cm (4 x 4 in) cm over stitch pattern

The gauge is not essential for this project but will impact the size of the project and yarn usage.

Stitch guide

Single crochet (sc)- insert hook in the next st, yrh, pull up a lp, yrh, pull through 2 lp on hook.

Crochet Blankets, Afghans And Throws

Foundation single crochet (fsc) – ch 2, insert hook in the second ch from hook, yrh, pull up a lp, yrh, pull through 1 lp on hook (ch made), yrh, pull through 2 lps (sc made), *insert hook in ch of previous st and pull up lp, yrh, pull through 1 lp (ch made), yrh, pull through 2 lps (sc made); rep from * until required number of fsc have been made.

First linked treble crochet (fltr) – ch 2, insert hook in back bump of 1st ch from hook, yrh and pull up lp (2 lps on hook), insert hook in back bump of 2nd ch from hook, yrh and pull up lp (3 lps o hook), insert hook in 1st st, yrh and pull up lp (4 lps on hook), [yrh and pull through 2 lps] 3 times.

Linked treble crochet (ltr) – insert hook from top to bottom through top front horizontal bar of previous st, yrh and pull up lp (2 lps on hook), insert hook from top to bottom through next horizontal bar of previous st, yrh and pull up lp (3 lps on hook), insert hook in next st, yrh and pull up lp (4 lps on hook), [yrh and pull through 2 lps] 3 times.

Bobble (bo) – yrh, insert hook in next, yrh and pull up lp, yrh and pull through 2 lps, [yrh, insert hook in same, yrh and pull up lp, yrh and pull through 2 lps] 4 times, yrh and pull through all 6 lps.

First star stitch (fstr) – ch 3, insert hook in the back bump of 2nd ch from hook, yrh and pull up lp (2 lps on hook), insert hook in the back bump of 3rd ch from hook, yrh and pull up lp (3 lps on hook), insert hook into 1st st, yrh and pull up lp (4 lps on hook), [insert hook into next st, yrh and pull up loop] twice (6 lps on hook), yrh and pull through all 6 lps.

Star stitch (str) – insert hook into lp that closed previous str, yrh and pull up lp (2 lps on hook), insert hook under 2 threads of last lp of previous str, yrh and pull up lp (3 lps on hook), insert hook into the same place as last lp of previous str, yrh and pull up lp (4 lps on hook), [insert hook into next st, yrh and pull up a lp] twice (6 lps on hook), yrh and pull through all 6 lps.

Notes

Similar worsted weight yarns may be substituted; please check gauge.

Beginning ch-1 does NOT count as stitch.

Instructions

Throw

Row 1 (WS): With **A**, fsc 143, turn. 143 sc.

Row 2 (RS): Fltr, ltr in each st across, turn. 143 ltr.

Row 3: Ch 1, sc in each st across to last st, insert hook in last st, yrh and pull through, drop **A**, yrh with **B** and pull through 2 lps, continue with **B**, turn.

Row 4: Ch 1, sc in the first st and next st, *bo in next st, sc in next st; rep from * to last st, insert hook in last st, yrh and pull through, drop **B**, yrh with **A** and pull through 2 lps, continue with **A**, turn.

Row 5: Ch 1, sc in each st across, turn.

Row 6: Repeat Row 2.

Row 7: Ch 1, sc in each st across to last, insert hook in last st, yrh and pull through, drop **A**, yrh with **C** and pull through 2 lps, continue with **C**, turn.

Row 8: Fstr, ch 1, *str, ch 1, rep from * to last st, sc in last st, turn.

Row 9: Ch 1, sc in each st across, turn.

Row 10-11: Repeat Rows 8-9.

Row 12: Fstr, ch 1, * str, ch 1; rep from * to last st, insert hook in last st, yrh and pull through, drop **C**, yrh with **A** and pull through 2 lps, continue with **A**, turn.

Row 13: Repeat Row 5.

Rows 14-18: Repeat Rows 2-6.

Row 19: Rep Row 5.

Rows 20- 127: Repeat Rows 2-19.

Fasten off.

Border

Round 1: With **C** sc evenly around edge placing [sc, ch 1, sc] in each corner. Ensure there are odd number of sc between consecutive corner ch-1 sp.

Round 2: Repeat Round 1.

Round 3: With **B** [Sc in 1st after corner ch-1 sp, *bo in next, sc in next, repeat from * to next corner ch-1 sp, [sc, ch 1, sc] in ch-1 sp] 4 times.

Rounds 4-5: Repeat Round 1.

Fasten off, weave in ends.

Finishing

Weave in ends and block to final measurements.

Falling Petals Afghan

Materials

Crochet Blankets, Afghans And Throws

Worsted weight yarn. The sample afghan was made with Lion Brand Pound of Love in colors Oxford Grey and Vintage White along with Lion Brand Heartland in color Yosemite.

Hook J(6mm).

Tapestry needle to weave in the ends.

Finished Size

36 inches wide and 42 inches long. You can make it any size you want. Instructions are included to adjust your foundation chain.

Gauge

5 Pattern Repeats= 6 inches

3 Rows= 4 1/4 inches

Yardage

Each stripe took 350 yards of yarn. I had 2 stripes of grey and cream, so it took 700 yards each. I had only a single stripe of the brown or coffee color. So it took only 350 yards. Each stripe is 36 inches wide and 8 1/2 inches tall. If you plan on adding one more stripe and making your afghan 50 inches, double the yardage for the coffee color.

Stitch abbreviations

ch-chain

dc-double crochet

fpdc-front post double crochet

Stitch Explanation

V st: (1 dc, ch 2, 1 dc) worked into the same st.

Shell St: (3 dc, ch 2, 3dc) worked into the same ch-2 space.

Directions

Ch 123. The initial chain is a multiple of 4 plus 3. If you want your afghan to be wider, chain any multiple of 4 and add an extra 3 chs. Every 4 chains will add about 1 1/4 inch to the width.

Crochet Blankets, Afghans And Throws

Row 1 Completed

Row 1: 1 V-st in the 5th ch from hook, *(sk the next 3 chs, 1 V-st in next), repeat from * to the last 2 sts, sk next st, 1 dc in the last st, turn.———30 V-sts

Row 2 Completed

Row 2: Ch 2, *(1 fpdc in the next dc (the first leg of your V-st), shell in the next ch-2 space, 1 fpdc in next dc (the second leg of your V-st), repeat from * to end, 1 dc on top of beginning ch 3, turn.——— 30 shells

Crochet Blankets, Afghans And Throws

Row 3 Completed

Row 3: Ch 2, 1 V-st in the ch-2 space of the next shell and each shell across to end, 1 dc on top of beginning ch2, turn. You will be skipping a lot of stitches to work your V's and that is what makes your shell stitches pop and look like petals.———30 V-sts

Repeat rows 2 and 3 until you have 6 shell rows and join the next color. Continue the stitch pattern repeating these two rows and changing colors after every 6th shell row. Your last row should be a shell row.

Adding Shells to the Foundation Chain Side

Once you finish your Afghan, you will see that your last row has a scalloped edge from the shells while your foundation chain side is straight. If you prefer, you can add shells to the foundation chain side as follows.

Notes

1. If you opt to add shells, you might want to add one more V-st and shell row to the very last stripe. This is because once you add the shells to teh foundation ch side, your first stripe will look wider than your last stripe.

2. We won't be working front post stitches for this row as it will add bulk to the fabric.

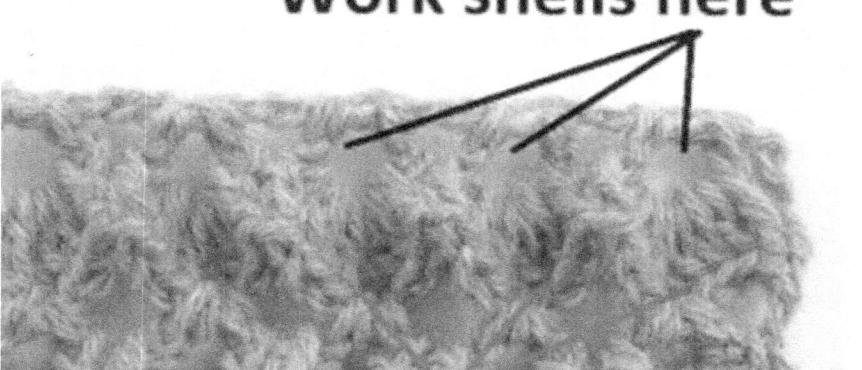

Shell Edging: With the right side of your blanket facing up, sl st to the corner of your foundation ch side using the same color yarn as the first row.

Ch 2, (3dc, ch2, 3dc)in the gap under the first shell and under each shell across to end, end with a dc in the last st. Fasten off.

Finishing

Fasten off and weave in any tails left.

Crochet Blankets, Afghans And Throws

5 Hour Blanket

Materials

Crochet Blankets, Afghans And Throws

Super Bulky, Size 6 Chenille yarn. Bernat Blanket yarn in colors Dark Grey, Vintage White and Bernat Baby Blanket in color Shell Pink was used for the sample blanket.

Size N/P(10mm) hook

Size K(6.5 mm) hook to weave in the ends.

Finished Size

32 X 39 inches when laid flat.

Yardage

1 skein each of the 3 colors. Each skein had 220 yards. I used almost all of the cream color and 170 yards of the grey and pink.

Stitch Abbreviations

ch-chain

ch space- chain space

sc-single crochet

Crochet Blankets, Afghans And Throws

esc- extended single crochet

beg ch- beginning chain

Stitch Explanations

Extended Single crochet (esc): Insert your hook into the next st and pull up a loop, yarn over and pull through one loop, yarn over again and pull through the remaining 2 loops on hook.——1 esc completed

Gauge

5 esc sts= 5 inches

Directions

With the cream color yarn, Ch 60. You can ch any even number to increase the width of your blanket.

Row 1 (work this row tight): 1 sc in 2nd ch from hook and each ch across. Turn.—-59 sc

Row 2: Ch 3 (counts as an esc+ ch 1), sk next st, esc in next, *(ch 1, sk next st, esc in next), repeat from * to end. Turn.———-30 esc

Note: At the end of Row 3, I found that working your last st into the beginning ch 1 gave a straighter edge compared to working into beg ch-2.

Row 3: Ch 2 (counts as esc), esc in adjacent ch-space, *(ch 1, sk next esc, esc in the next ch-space), repeat from * until you work an esc in the ch-space under beg ch-3, esc on top of beg ch-1. Turn.——-31 esc

Row 4: Ch 3 (counts as esc+ ch 1), sk next st, 1 esc in next ch-space, *(ch 1, sk next st, 1 esc in next ch-space), repeat from * to last 2 sts (esc+beg ch), ch 1, sk next esc, 1 esc on top of beginning ch-2, join pink color yarn, fasten off the cream color. Turn.———-30 esc

Note: You will alternate between Rows 3 and 4 with color changes in between.

Row 5: Repeat Row 3 in color pink, join color grey at the end of the row, and fasten off the pink. Turn.

Row 6: Repeat Row 4 in color grey, join color cream at the end of the row and fasten off the grey. Turn.

Row 7: Repeat Row 3 in color cream, join color pink at the end of the row, and fasten off the cream. Turn.

Row 8: Repeat Row 4 in color pink, join color cream at the end of the row, and fasten off the pink. Turn.

Row 9- 23: Repeat Rows 3 and 4 alternately in color cream, join color pink at the end of Row 23, and fasten off the color cream. Turn.

Notes

1. If you want to adjust the length of your blanket, you can crochet more or fewer rows here, but remember to write the number of rows down for the remaining two panels.

2. My cream panel now measured approximately 9 1/2 inches from the top of the pink row.

Row 24-38: Repeat Rows 4 and 3 in color pink for the next 15 rows, join color grey at the end of Row 38, fasten off the color pink. Turn.

Row 39-53: Repeat Rows 3 and 4 in color grey for the next 15 rows, join color pink at the end of Row 53, fasten off the color grey. Turn.

Row 54: Repeat Row 4 in color pink, join color cream at the end of the row and fasten off the color pink. Turn.

Row 55: Repeat Row 3 in color cream, join grey at the end of the row and fasten off the color cream. Turn.

Row 56: Repeat Row 4 in color grey, join pink at the end of the row and fasten off the color grey. Turn.

ROw 57: Repeat Row 3 in color pink, join cream at the end of the row and fasten off the pink. Turn.

Row 58-60: Repeat Row 4, 3 and 4 again in color cream. Turn

Row 61: Continuing with cream color, ch 2 (counts as a hdc), 1 hdc in each ch and st across to end, fasten off.—-60 hdc

Note: The last Row is a hdc row and not a single crochet row like the first row because the hdc made it the same width as the first colorful panel.

Finishing

Using the smaller hook, weave in all the tails left. Take care to weave in through the top part of your esc sts to avoid your tails showing through the gaps.

Little Lily Baby Blanket

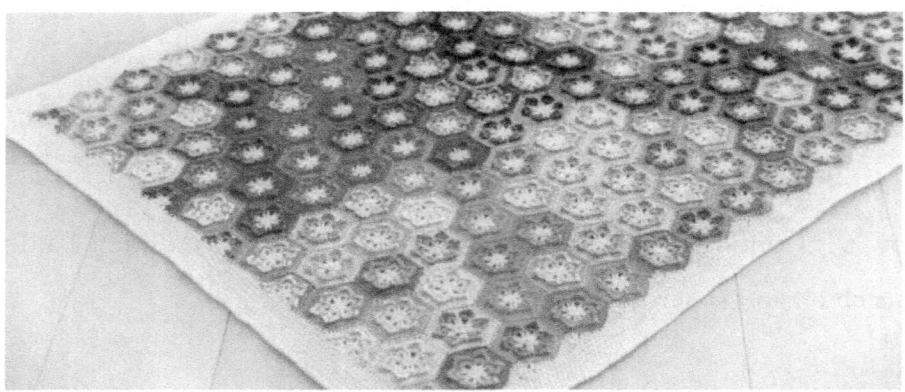

Materials:

Scheepjes Catona (100% mercerised cotton, 100g/250m)

Colour A: 106 Snow White x 3 balls

Scheepjes Catona colour pack (109 x 10g balls)

Full pack: x 109 balls

Crochet hook

3.5mm (US Size E/4).

Crochet Blankets, Afghans And Throws

Measurements

Blocked and finished blanket measures 91 x 115cm (36 x 45in).

Gauge/tension

Motif up to Round 5 measures 7cm (2.75in) across flat to flat side, 8cm (3.15in) across point to point.

Notes

You'll use different colours for each motif. These are indicated in the pattern as 'Colour 1' and 'Colour 2'. Check out the colour layout and table for the actual colour combinations. Please note that full motifs with combination 52 and 88 are only made once, all the other twice.

The motifs are joined together in Round 5 as-you-go.

Abbreviations

BPhdc: Back Post half double crochet: yarn over, insert hook from back to front and back to back around stem of st, yarn over, pull up loop, yarn over, pull through all loops

ch: chain

ch-sp: chain-space

dc: double crochet

dc2tog: double crochet 2 stitches together: (yarn over, insert hook in st/sp, yarn over, pull up loop, yarn over, pull through first 2 loops on hook) in each of the two sts/sps, yarn over, pull through all loops on hook

dc3tog: double crochet 3 stitches together: (yarn over, insert hook in st/sp, yarn over, pull up loop, yarn over, pull through first 2 loops on hook) in each of the three sts/sps, yarn over, pull through all loops on hook

dc5tog: double crochet 5 stitches together: (yarn over, insert hook in st/sp, yarn over, pull up loop, yarn over, pull through first 2 loops on hook) in each of the five sts/sps, yarn over, pull through all loops on hook

dropped hdc: dropped half double crochet: yarn over, insert hook in indicated st/sp, yarn over, pull up loop, yarn over, pull through all loops on hook

hdc: half double crochet

picot: ch2, insert hook in second ch from hook, yarn over, pull up loop and immediately pull through loops on hook

RS: right side

sc: single crochet

sp(s): space(s)

ss: slip stitch

st(s): stitch(es)

WS: wrong side

Repeat formats

*....; rep from * once/twice/3x Crochet the instructions after * and then repeat that section a further number of times as indicated.

(...) once/twice/3x Crochet the instructions between brackets the total number of times indicated.

[...] Indicates the amount of stitches at the end of a row or round.

(…) in same st/sp Indicates that all instructions between brackets are worked in the same stitch or space.

Colour layout

Full motif colour combinations

You will create 182 full motifs and 13 half motifs with the colours from your colour pack. You'll need to make two full motifs out of each colour combination, with the exception of combination 88 and 52 where you'll only make one full motif.

Note that the colour combinations are paired: Combination 1 and 2 are both combining the same colours, only for two motifs Colour 1 is used on the inside, and for the other combination Colour 2. So while the table lists 92 combinations, you only have 46 pairs of colours. The numbers in the table below correspond with the numbers in the colour overview.

You will not use colour 74, 105, 106, 110, 130, 157, 162, 248, 254, 257, 387, 393, 395, 404, 501, 505 and 507.

Crochet Blankets, Afghans And Throws

Tip: Sort out your combinations at the start of the blanket and keep the balls together with a rubber band or something similar.

Half motif colour combinations

Make 1 half motif each with combination 19, 21, 23, 26, 28, 30, 34, 37, 41, 44, 50, 52 and 90. If you don't have enough yarn leftovers for these combinations, pick similar colours that are not used in adjacent motifs.

Colour Layout

Crochet Blankets, Afghans And Throws

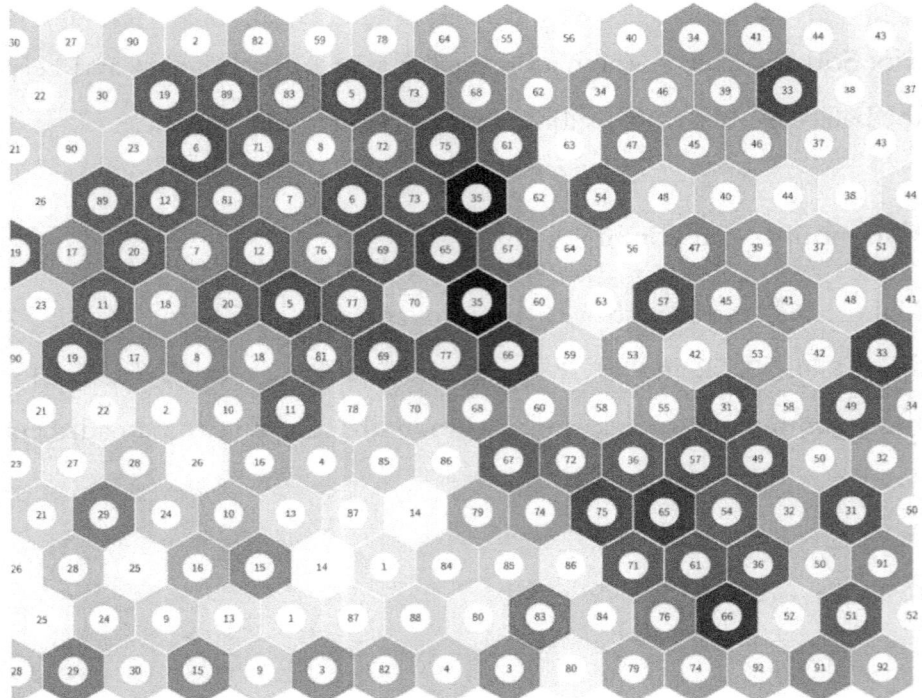

Techniques

Joining motifs

You'll be joining the motifs as you go in the final Round. We'll join with a flat join, which's achieved by taking the hook out of your loop and inserting it in the back loop of your opposite motif before picking it up again. This effectively slip stitches the motifs together.

After each join, you crochet a regular stitch, like you do when you're crocheting a motif's side.

When you join a new motif, you start with the corner. Remove your hook from your current (blue) loop. Insert it through the back loop of the second ch of the ch-sp of your opposite motif (photo 1, it's the loop on the side closest to you). Pick up your first loop again (photo 2), and pull through the loop on hook (photo 3).

Crochet Blankets, Afghans And Throws

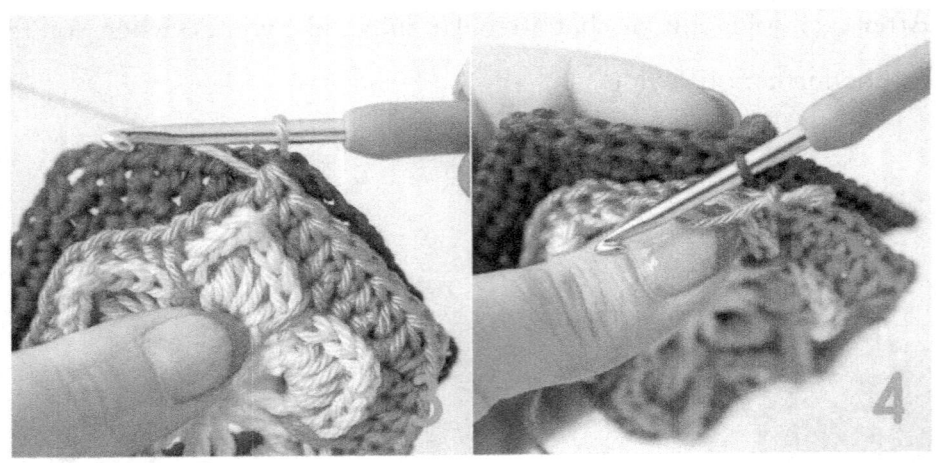

You've now got one blue loop on your hook, and your motifs are joined in one stitch. Ch1 (that's the other ch to form your corner), remove your hook from the blue loop, insert through the back loop of the next st on your other motif (photo 4), pick the first loop back up (photo 5) and pull through (photo 6), 1hdc in same st as your previous hdc, and that's your corner made!

Crochet Blankets, Afghans And Throws

Continue like this across the side for the next 7 sts Joining to the back loop of the opposite st before making your hdc (photos 8-10).

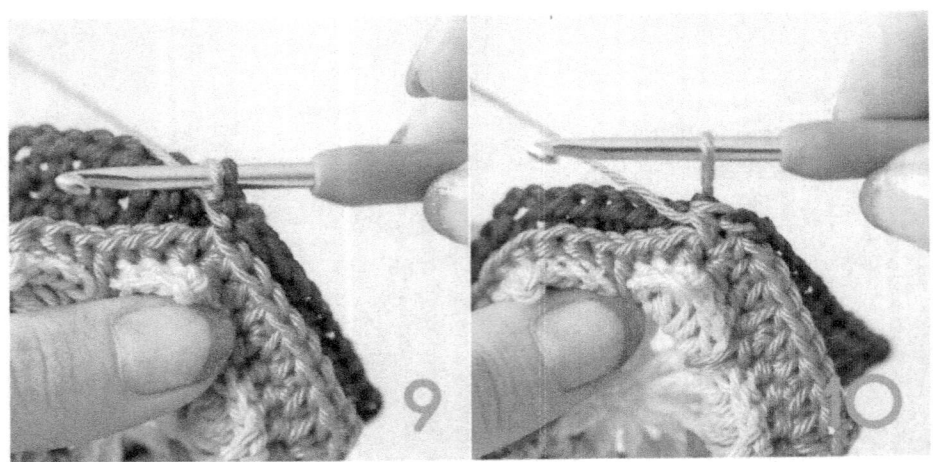

You now have 8 hdc made: one that's part of your first corner, six over the side of your motif and one that's the first hdc of your next corner. To finish up your second corner, ch1, join to back loop of first ch in the ch-sp of your other motif. That completes your side join (photo 11).

If there's another motif to join, work one ss in the join between the other two motifs and continue joining as above. If you're not joining another motif, follow the pattern instructions.

Instructions:

Motif (make 182)

The motifs are worked in rounds on the RS, no turning involved.

With Colour A, make a magic ring.

Round 1 (RS) 6sc in magic ring, ss in first sc, close ring by pulling thread. [6 sc]

Round 2 Ch4 (counts as first dc + ch1), 1dc in st at base of ch4, *(1dc, ch1, 1dc) in next st; repeat from * another 4 times, ss in third ch, cut yarn. [12 dc, 6 ch-sps]

Round 3 Join Colour 1 with a ss in the sp between 2 dc, ch1, 1sc in same sp, *(3dc, picot, 3dc) in next ch-1 sp, 1sc in next sp between 2 dc; repeat from * another 4 times, (3dc, picot, 3dc) in next ch-1 sp, ss in first sc, cut yarn. [36 dc, 6 picots, 6 sc]

Round 4 Join Colour 2 with a ss around the stem of st before a sc, ch2 (doesn't count as st), 1BPhdc in same st, 1 dropped hdc in sp between 2 dc in Round 2 (dropped hdc sits over sc of previous round), *1BPhdc around each of next 6 sts skipping picot, 1 dropped hdc in sp between 2 dc of Round 2; repeat from * another 4 times, 1BPhdc around each of next 5 sts skipping picot, ss in first BPhdc, don't cut yarn. [36 BPhdc, 6 dropped hdc]

You'll be joining the motifs in Round 5. Work the instructions below for the first motif. Follow the instructions for Round 5 in the 'Joining' chapter for every other motif.

Round 5 (First motif only) Ch2 (doesn't count as st), 1hdc in st at base of ch2, 4hdc, (1hdc, ch2, 1hdc) in next st, *6hdc, (1hdc, ch2, 1hdc) in next st; repeat from * another 4 times, 1hdc, ss in first hdc, cut yarn. [48 hdc, 6 ch-sps]

Weave in all ends. You can crochet over the ends of Round 1, 3 and 5 as you go if you don't want to weave in all the ends separately.

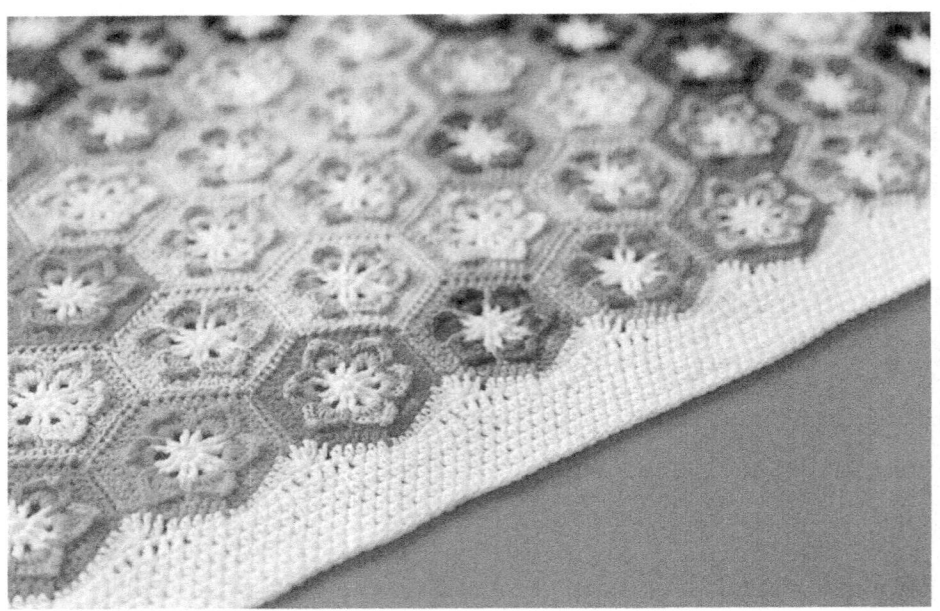

Half motif (make 13)

The half motif will be worked in rows. You will turn in the first row. All other rows are worked from the RS without turning. See Diagram 2: Half Motif for extra clarification.

With Colour A, make a magic ring.

Row 1 (WS) Ch1, 4sc in ring, don't close ring with ss as for whole motif but turn work, pull ring tight. [4 sc]

Row 2 (RS) Ch4 (counts as first dc + ch1), 1dc in sc at base of ch4, (1dc, ch1, 1dc) 3 times, cut yarn. [8 dc, 4 ch]

Row 3 (RS) Join Colour 1 with ss in the first ch-sp, (ch3, picot, 3dc) in ch-sp, *1sc between 2 dc from previous row, (3dc, picot, 3dc) in next ch-sp; repeat from * another time, 1sc between 2 dc from previous row, (3dc, picot, 1dc) in final ch-sp, cut yarn. [20 dc, 4 picots, 3 sc]

Row 4 (RS) Join Colour 2 with a ss in first ch-sp (to the right of the picot, so it will look like you're making a BPhdc around the ch3), ch2 (counts as first BPhdc), skip picot, 1BPhdc around each of next 3 dc's, 1 dropped hdc in sp between 2 dc's of Row 2 (dropped hdc sits over sc of previous row), *1BPhdc around each of next 6 sts skipping picot, 1 dropped hdc in sp between 2 dc's of Row 2; repeat from * another time, 1BPhdc around each of next 4 sts skipping picot, cut yarn. [20 BPhdc, 3 dropped hdc]

You'll be joining the half motifs in Row 5. Because you cut yarn between Row 4 and 5 anyway, You can find Row 5 joining instructions for the half motifs in the 'Joining' chapter below.

Weave in all ends.

Joining

You'll be joining the motifs as you go in its final Round. We'll join with a flat join. This is done as follows: remove your hook from the loop on your current motif, insert hook in the stitch on the other motif from front to back, pick up the loop again and pull through the stitch, effectively slip stitching the stitches together. After joining the stitch, you work a regular stitch like you would if you were crocheting a side.

This method gives you a flat and delicate finish. It is a little time consuming too. If you'd rather make a quick join, simply crochet the motifs together with ss's in each motif corner and skip the picking up of stitches.

You'll first be joining all full motifs. Once the blanket is assembled, you'll add the half motifs. Please note that the left corners have different joining instructions than the other half motifs due to their placement.

Joining Round 5 (RS) Ch2 (doesn't count as st), 1hdc in st at base of ch2, 4hdc, *(1hdc, ch2, 1hdc) in next st, 6hdc; repeat from * until you reach a side that needs to be joined to other motifs. 1hdc, ch1.

*Remove hook from loop, pick up back loop from second ch in corner of other motif, pick up loop from original motif, pull through. You've now joined to the other motif with what's basically a ss in the back loop. Ch1, remove loop from hook, pick up back loop of the next st on the other motif (this is the first hdc), pick up loop again and pull through, 1hdc in corner-st on original motif (the st where you've also made your last hdc). You finished your first joined corner space.

Crochet Blankets, Afghans And Throws

Continue across side of motif by working (join to back loop of st on other motif, 1hdc) 7 times, join to back loop of next st on other motif, ch1, ss in join/ch, ch1, join to back loop of first hdc on next motif, 1hdc in corner-st of motif, (join to back loop of st on other motif, 1hdc) 7 times, join to back loop of next st on other motif, ch1, ss in join/ch, ch1; If you need to join another side, repeat from * to ; another time. If you've reached a non-joined side, 1hdc in same st as last hdc to create corner, 1hdc, ss in first hdc, cut yarn. [48 hdc, 6 ch-sps]

Joining troubleshooting

It happens occasionally that one side of the motif has more stitches than the other. Usually it means that you've crocheted sts in the corner space of Round 3 or 4. You can either redo the motif, or improvise a little bit in Round 5 by crocheting sts together on the short side, and working multiple sts in one st on the long side.

Joining half motifs

The half motifs are joined over their short sides to other motifs. Please note that the instructions for the left upper corner and left bottom corner half motifs differ from the general instructions. They're specified below.

Joining Row 5 (RS) Join Colour 2 with a ss in second ch from beg-ch of previous row, ch2, ss in ch-sp of other motif, ch1, (join to back loop of st on other motif, 1hdc) 8 times, join to back loop of next st on other motif, ch1, ss in join/ch, ch1.

Pick up back loop of ch on next motif, 1hdc in same st as last hdc to create corner, (join to back loop of st on other motif, 1hdc) 7 times, join to back loop of next st on other motif, ch1, ss in join/ch, ch1.

Pick up back loop of second ch on next motif, 1hdc in same st as last hdc to create corner, (join to back loop of st on other motif, 1hdc) 7 times, join to back loop of next st on other motif, ch1, ss in join/ch, ch1, 1hdc in same st as prev hdc. Cut yarn. [26 hdc, 4 ch-2 corners]

Left upper corner half motif (colour combo 30)

Note: The final side of this motif does not have an adjacent motif.

Joining Round (RS) Join Colour A with a ss in the most right ch-sp, ch2, ss in ch-sp of other motif, join sides as for full motif. When you've worked the ss in the final corner, ch1, 1hdc in same st as corner hdc, 7hdc, ch1, 1hdc in final st. Cut yarn.

Left bottom corner half motif (colour combo 28)

Note: The first side of this motif does not have an adjacent motif.

Joining Round (RS) Join Colour A with a ss in the most right ch-sp, ch2, 7hdc, 1hdc in final st on side, ch1, ss in other ch-sp, continue joining as for other half motifs. Cut yarn.

Edge

The first couple of rounds are a mixture of different stitches with different heights. This is so we can fill up the gaps on the long sides of the blanket. It might look complicated, but once you get into the rhythm of the stitches it will make sense. Have a look at Diagram 3: Edge Rounds 1-4 for some visual help.

Round 1 (RS) Join Colour A with a ss in the left upper corner (orange/brown half motif), ch2 (counts as first hdc), *14hdc divided evenly over long side motif, 8hdc in next motif, 1hdc in last ch-sp of motif; repeat from * another 5 times, 14hdc divided evenly over long side motif, 1hdc in last ch-sp, ch2, rotate blanket 90 degrees.

1sc in corner-sp, *2sc, 3hdc, 1dc, dc5tog in next 2 sts, join and next 2 sts on other motif while skipping the ch -sp's, 1dc, 3hdc, 2sc, 1sc in ch-sp; repeat from * another 13 times, 2sc, 3hdc, 1dc, dc2tog in last 2 sts, 1dc in corner-sp, ch2, rotate blanket 90 degrees.

1hdc in corner-sp, *8hdc in next motif, 1hdc in last ch-sp of motif; 14hdc divided evenly over long side motif; repeat from * another 5 times, 8hdc in next motif, 1hdc in corner-sp, ch2, rotate blanket 90 degrees.

1dc in ch-sp, dc2tog in first 2 sts, 1dc, 3hdc, 2sc, 1sc in ch-sp, *2sc, 3hdc, 1dc, dc5tog in next 2 sts, join and next 2 sts on other motif while skipping the ch-sp's, 1dc, 3hdc, 2sc, 1sc in ch-sp; repeat from * another 13 times, ch2, join with ss in beg-ch2, cut yarn. [First short side 154 sts, long sides 205 sts, second short side 148 sts]

Round 2 (RS) Join Colour A with a ss in the left upper corner, ch2 (counts as first hdc), 1hdc in each st to corner-sp, 1hdc in corner-sp, rotate blanket 90 degrees.

1sc in corner-sp, *sc2tog, 3hdc, 2dc, dc2tog in dc5tog and next st, 2dc, 3hdc; repeat from * another 13 times, sc2tog, 3hdc, 2dc, dc2tog, 1dc in ch-sp, ch2, rotate blanket 90 degrees.

1hdc in corner-sp, 1hdc in each st to end, 1hdc in corner-sp, ch2, rotate blanket 90 degrees.

1dc in corner-sp, dc3tog, 2dc, 3hdc, *sc2tog, 3hdc, 2dc, dc2tog in dc5tog and next st, 2dc, 3hdc; repeat from * another 13 times, 1sc in last st, 1sc in corner-sp, ch2, join to first st. [First short side 156 sts, long sides 177 sts, second short side 150 sts]

Round 3 (RS) Join Colour A with a ss in the left upper corner, ch2 (counts as first hdc), *1hdc in each st to end, (1hdc, ch2 1hdc) in ch-sp; repeat from * another 2 times, 1hdc in each st to end, 1hdc in ch-sp, ch2, join to first st. cut yarn. [First short side 158 sts, long sides 178 sts, second short side 152 sts]

The edge should almost lay completely flat at this point. If it instead waves, it means that you have more sts in the edge than 'space' available. To counter this, check where your blanket waves (this is often on the long sides, above the ch-sps of motifs), and mark with stitch markers if necessary on Round 2. Next, rip out Round 3 and decrease by crocheting either a hdc2tog or dc2tog on the indicated spaces. If need be, work extra decreases in the upcoming rounds.

Rounds 4-8 Join Colour A with a ss in the left upper corner, ch2 (counts as first hdc), *1hdc in each st to corner-sp, (2hdc, ch2, 1hdc) in corner-sp; repeat from * another 2 times, 1hdc in each st to corner-sp, 2hdc, ch2, join with ss in first st, cut yarn. [First short side 173 sts, long sides 193 sts, second short side 167 sts]

Because we're working in rounds and the stitches are slightly slanted, this would eventually cause your corners to become rounded because of excessive pulling on one side of the corner. By making 2hdc in the corner-sp at the end of each side you'll offset this. However, if you feel that you only need 1hdc feel free to adjust.

Weave in all ends and block the blanket to size.

Made in United States
Orlando, FL
06 February 2024

43367509R00046